LET'S PLAY! LITTLE CHAMPS

TABLE TENNIS

KIM THOMPSON

NorwoodHouse Press

Cataloging-in-Publication Data

Names: Thompson, Kim, 1970-.
Title: Table tennis / Kim Thompson.
Description: Buffalo, NY : Norwood House Press, 2026. | Series: Let's play! little champs | Includes glossary and index.
Identifiers: ISBN 9781978577220 (pbk.) | ISBN 9781978577237 (library bound) | ISBN 9781978577244 (ebook)
Subjects: LCSH: Table tennis--Juvenile literature.
Classification: LCC GV1005.T474 2026 | DDC 796.346--dc23

Published in 2026 by
Norwood House Press
2544 Clinton Street
Buffalo, NY 14224

Designer: Rhea Magaro

Photo credits: Cover, pp. 1, 15 Torychemistry/Shutterstock.com; p. 5 DarioZg/Shutterstock.com; p. 6 muzsy/Shutterstock.com; p. 7 Dmytro Zinkevych/Shutterstock.com; p. 9 Andrew Angelov/Shutterstock.com; pp. 10, 13, 18 niktalena/Shutterstock.com; p. 11 Paha_l/Dreamstime.com; p. 14 Sergey Novikov/Shutterstock.com; p. 16 Fotokostic/ Shutterstock.com; pp. 17, 19 AYO Production/Shutterstock.com; p. 21 3445128471/Shutterstock.com

Printed in the United States of America

CPSIA compliance information: Batch #CWNHP26: For further information contact Norwood House Press at 1-800-237-9932.

TABLE OF CONTENTS

What Is Table Tennis?

Table tennis is a fun sport. It is popular all over the world. It is even played at the Olympics.

It may seem like players don't move much. This is false! Table tennis is active and fast-paced.

It builds strength and **flexibility**. It provides **aerobic exercise**. It also improves **hand-eye coordination**.

The Gear

Players need a table with a net. If they don't have one at home, they can find a table at a community center.

Each player needs a **paddle**. It's good to have a supply of balls.

Table tennis players need lots of practice. Special gear can help.

A training robot launches balls from different angles. Players can practice hitting each ball.

Table tennis players need light, comfortable clothing and flexible shoes. They keep a towel and water bottle close by.

At the Table

Singles table tennis is for two players. Doubles is for four players.

Games are played to 11 points. **Matches** are won by winning three out of five games. Players score points when **opponents** are unable to return the ball.

Skills and Techniques

Players use a **stance** in which their feet are apart and their knees are bent. This keeps them ready to make quick movements.

Players take turns **serving**. They try to make the ball bounce on their side of the table before it goes over the net and bounces on the other side.

Forehand and backhand strokes are used to return serves and hit balls over the net.

In a forehand stroke, right-handers hit the ball from their right side. Left-handers hit from their left side. For a backhand, the arm is turned across the body.

How to Be Match-Ready

Players should eat healthy foods like fruits, vegetables, and lean meats. They should drink plenty of water. Getting enough sleep keeps them alert and ready to play.

GLOSSARY

aerobic exercise (air-OH-bik EK-sur-size): moving your body in a way that makes your heart beat faster and your lungs work harder to keep you healthy and strong

flexibility (FLEK-suh-bil-i-tee): the ability to bend easily

hand-eye coordination (hand-eye koh-or-duh-NAY-shuhn): being able to use your hands and eyes together to catch, hit, or throw things accurately

matches (MAT-chis): complete competitions that are made up of several smaller games

opponents (uh-POH-nuhnts): the people you are playing against in a game or sport

paddle (PAD-uhl): the flat tool with a handle that you use to hit the ball in table tennis

serving (SUR-ving): hitting the ball to begin play

stance (stans): the way you position your body and feet when you are ready to play

THINKING QUESTIONS

1. Why is table tennis good for you?

2. What do you need to play table tennis?

3. What is a training robot?

4. How do you score points in table tennis?

5. What does it mean to serve the ball?

INDEX

ABOUT THE AUTHOR

Kim Thompson is a writer, mom, and sports fan from Columbus, Ohio. She loves to watch athletes' amazing skills on the court, field, or diamond. She believes that all kids should try out the sports that interest them and always remember to have fun!